# Can we be

# HONEST

## about

# MONEY?

Creating a New
Generation of Millionaires

**BY:**

**MICHAEL A. BEMPAH**

**DISCLAIMER!** All investments involve risk, and the past performance of a security, industry, sector, market, financial product, trading strategy, or individual's trading does not guarantee future results or returns. Investors are fully responsible for any investment decisions they make. Such decisions should be based solely on evaluation of one's own financial circumstances, investment objectives, risk tolerance, liquidity, and in-depth research of the security.

# CONTENTS

## STOCK TRADING

It's your favorite stock investor, Michael A. Bempah, and author of Can We Be Honest About Money. Can We Be Honest About Money, was written to get more individuals involved with investing and to break down why it's important to budget, save, and invest for your future. No matter where you are in life, financial literacy is the key to obtaining generational wealth.

Many of us took the route of higher education only to realize it doesn't guarantee a high paying career and/or financial freedom. Even those with degrees still find themselves struggling with the cost of living which has now reached extreme levels. The best way known to man to offset inflation is investing in the stock market. So that's just what I did.

I started by taking a look at my network's 401k accounts to see what kind of returns we were making. I knew mine wasn't profitable but I thought, maybe, my colleagues were having better success. Come to find out, we were all in the same boat having little to no profit from our 401k accounts.

Next, I began to research all of the "stock market trader" turned "millionaire" to see what strategies they used for successful trading. I learned they all had their own unique trading strategies. I, then, invested money into classes to learn what the "professionals" were teaching. That was a little helpful but not worth the tuition prices charged.

I know this sounds like a lot, and it was, but it was necessary. Truthfully, the best teacher is experience. I could have saved so much time and money if I could find all of the right information in one place. I was getting bits and pieces from the instructors. There is a lot of misleading information out there and it can be intimidating and confusing. I created this short and easy to read guide so you will have the confidence to create a strategy and place your first trade.

*Can We Be Honest About Money*, was written to get more individuals involved in investing and to break down why it's important to budget, save, and invest for your future. *Can We Be Honest About Money* is focused on transforming the way you view your money and your finances. This book will explore the many tactics used to keep you blind when it comes to attaining financial freedom.

In, *Can We Be Honest About Money*, I also focus on stock trading. Investing in stocks is a great way to build wealth. The hardest part when starting to invest is sorting through the massive amount of information that's available which can be very intimidating and often misleading. I want to give you what I feel is important so you can begin trading stocks with confidence.

Lastly, I will discuss Option Trading. Options trading is an income-based strategy for those looking to make a little extra money. It can also be used as insurance to protect your stock. In this book, you will learn what options are and some of the ways you can use it to your advantage to achieve your goals. Learn to make your money grow with this short book on budgeting, saving, and stock trading. Use this book as a guide as well as motivation to starting your journey to financial freedom. If you're ready for your money to start working for you, let's begin.

# CHAPTER 1:

# TRUTH ABOUT SALES
## *[BUDGETING AND SAVING]*

G aining financial freedom requires discipline and good habits just like anything else something in life. From as difficult something requires as discipline as losing simple weight. and as waking good It requires up habits on time a just positive to like go attitude, a game plan, and consistency.

Now, there is nothing wrong with liking nice things. I, too, am guilty of that. But the problems occur when you begin to get carried away and spend outside of your means. It's not your fault. There are tons of psychology studies that goes into sales and marketing strategies to get you to spend your money.

Have you ever received a sales paper and saw an item that you "forgot" you needed? If you hadn't seen the item in the paper would you have bought it or even remembered that you needed it? That's just one trick out of thousands that are used to drain your bank account.

Another thing I hear a lot is, "I work hard enough to buy what I want." You convince yourself even though you know you're spending money unnecessarily. The next time you say this to yourself, walk away and give yourself at least a month. If you still want that item after a month go ahead and buy it. I believe in following your heart, but I don't believe in impulse spending.

Another major trick that causes people to over spend is the conversion from cash to debit cards. With a debit card, it's easier to lose track of those smaller daily purchases. It's also easier to make a big purchase without thumbing through a lot of cash which might give you doubt on spending that amount of money in the first place.

When you begin to connect the dots, and you realize, it's not how much money you make; it's how much money you can save. Then you connect it with investing to make your money grow. MB-University is here to turn that light bulb on and let the ideas and creative juices flow. What's the end goal and how do you get there?

I've taken business classes and I was surprised to learn how much money most companies spend to strategize on a certain demographics lack of knowledge. These companies take advantage of certain groups of people weaknesses to gain advantage. Let's educate ourselves on the many tactics used to keep up spending money in order to gain financial freedom.

# CHAPTER 2:

# REDUCING SPENDING & GETTING OUT OF DEBT
## *[BUDGETING AND SAVINGS]*

I have worked as a financial advisor for doctors and lawyers and they, too, encounter the same problems as the average individual. They are working with a fixed income and the pressure from their peers to maintain a certain standard of living. They deal with the pressure of driving nice cars and having nice homes. They are in this "prestigious role" where they can't look cheap and challenge charges like a $200 oil change.

This is a universal problem but if you make up your mind to save money and invest you will get much further than the individuals earning a 6-figure salary. Cut that phone bill in half, reduce your cable package, start cooking more often, limit the days you go out per week. These changes will save you hundreds a month and I'll teach you how to turn these hundreds into thousands.

Being poor is more of a state of mind than anything. Most people want to keep up with the Joneses, so they buy the latest and newest items just to say they have it. The item is usually a topic of discussion or brings them some type of attention. You're paying extra money for this feeling.

The newest phones cost approximately $200 more than a 6-month older version. Does it make sense to pay $200 more? To most people, it does. This is playing into the psychology of economic status. If you spend more, you're worth more, which is also false. To be worth more you have to have money and/or assets that appreciate in value.

If I were to give you $10,000 right now I'm sure you can tell me a few different ways you could spend it, but can you tell me a few different ways you can invest it? What kind of profit will you make from your investment? You probably don't know right off the top of your head and if you say 401Ks, CDs or mutual funds then you're just wasting your time.

These investments don't give you any real return on your money. What if I can give you a simple way of creating long-term wealth and generating weekly income? That's what I intend to show you but first, we have to break the mental chain.

# CHAPTER 3:

# CREATING A BUDGET
## *[BUDGETING AND SAVING]*

C reating a budget is a basic and fundamental skill that we should all be taught at home however most often we are not. It's easier than it seems. The first step is writing everything you purchase down in a notebook. This all gives you a good idea of how much money you spend on a daily, weekly, and monthly basis. From there, you can create a budget. This budget will consist of fixed bills and flexible bills.

Fixed bills can be anything from rent to insurance. They are bills that don't change. Flexible bills can be anything from gas, groceries, to pocket money. These are bills that change and varies from month to month. So be sure to overestimate a little bit on flexible bills. The reason you want to overestimate is because your rather have too much money when your spending than too little money.

Last but not least, remember to pay yourself first. I know this seems like a backwards concept but you work hard for your money. You must see some kind of reward in what you are doing. When you pay yourself first, you begin to put yourself first. Your bills become second to you, your goals, and your future. For beginners, I recommend giving yourself at least 10% of your monthly income. This will be money you will begin to invest.

Before any of this can happen, you must make a concrete decision that you will get out of debt not next week, not next year, but now.

Let's go over an example budget. Let's say you make $2,700 a month. The first thing you need to do is pay yourself 10%. 10% of $2,700 is $270. This is the money we will

use to invest. Next, make two columns. One column for fixed bills and the next column for flexible bills.

Your fixed bills will be rent and all the other bills that don't change in value. So, let's say for example your rent is $800, you have a car note that's $300, insurance $80, cable bill $90, utilities $160, a cell phone bill $100. These fixed bills total to $1,530.

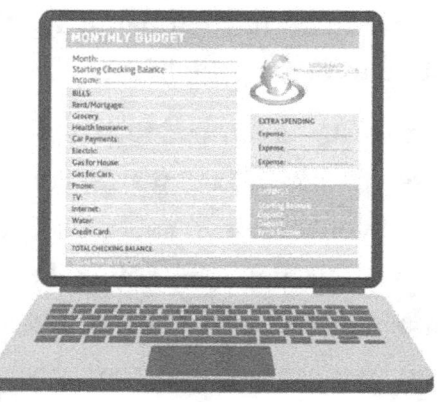

This image shows a basic breakdown of your weekly bills. The idea is to keep track of all the money you spend. From there, you can figure out ways to save more money. This is the foundation, and the answer to the questions like, how much money do I need to start investing?

In your flexible bill column, you have groceries $320, gas for your vehicle $200 a month, entertainment money, another $200 a month. These bills in your flexible column bill total to $720. $1,530 + $720 is $2,250.

You make $2,700 a month minus the $2,250, it leaves you with $450. You can put $450 in your savings but you don't have to. Remember, you have to put $270 of that into your savings. $180 can be used just for miscellaneous spending, and if nothing else comes up, I recommend you put in your savings as well.

There are other examples online and spreadsheets you can use and download to create a budget for yourself. Creating a budget is the first and most important step towards investing. Review this chapter over and over again until you get the hang of it.

# CHAPTER 4:

# TRUTH ABOUT BANKS AND WHY YOU SHOULD INVEST
## [BUDGETING AND SAVING]

Have you ever wondered why banks pay you to open an account with direct deposits? Banks invest your money on a short-term and a long-term basis. If you have a savings account and you make too many withdrawals they hit you with fees because they have a system of investing.

You can put your money in CDs where you'll get a better rate of return but it's locked in and untouchable for years while they invest your money in the market to make millions, they use your money and your peers' money to issue loans for homes, cars, and businesses.

The Federal Reserve mandates the bank keep 10% of your money available in cash for withdrawal. If you want to withdraw $5,000, the bank has no problem with giving you your money but if you want to withdraw $5 Million, depending on where you live, they may ask you to come back at a later date because they don't have the money on site. That other 90% is invested in the stock market where they trade stocks, futures, forex and government bonds.

The banks make billions from the small direct deposit accounts you open because they utilize your funds on a back-end while showing you it's available for withdrawal on the front-end. They have it down to a science. Every time your direct deposit hits your account, the banks are investing 80% of your money into the stock market.

The banks have a system of utilization so by the third day most of your money is ready for withdrawal. That's when the banks are done investing in the stock market.

# CHAPTER 5:

# CREDIT AND LEVERAGE
## *[BUDGETING AND SAVING]*

I have a chapter where I talk about getting out of debt. That's referring to small petty debts like credit cards and even car loans. If you want to hurt your credit do it for big money. That's my motto.

Some debts are good debts like a mortgage because it gives you leverage. Leverage in the investment world means to control a lot with a little. For example, with good credit, I can buy a house that cost $150,000 with only $3,000 down and a signature. Then I can turn around and sell that same house for $200,000. That $3,000 and a signature, made me $50,000. You can easily do that in a stock market trading forex, futures, and options. Build your credit to take advantage of the benefits of leverage which increases buying power.

# CHAPTER 6:

# TRUTH ABOUT 401K
## *[STOCK TRADING]*

W hat got me started in trading is the fact that for many years I had a 401K. I didn't pay much attention to it until one day I had a talk with my uncle about investing. He made it clear to me that it was a major part of him obtaining wealth. One day, I was sitting at home with my 401K statement and saw that I lost over $2,000 that quarter. There were no minus signs only parenthesis which is a nice way in the financial world of saying you lost money.

So, I called the investment firm for some answers. I wanted to know which stock my money was invested in. All they could tell me was that I was in a 30-year retirement fund plan. They couldn't tell me which stocks or bonds my money was in so I asked to speak to a manager.

Check your 401K and determine if you are making a good return from your contribution. Consider the time frame as well as what stock and bonds are within your portfolio. Just imagine, if you take the time to learn the basics, you can and will yield a greater return then your 401k.

The manager did not have a clue about where my money was invested either. This is what prompted me to learn on my own how to invest. As I learned more and more and as I spoke with financial advisors I realized that their job is not to invest my money but to make me feel comfortable about investing. Whether the market goes up or down they must invest my money. In return, they get to charge me fees.

They also get money by leasing my stock out like real estate by utilizing options. This is a huge part of the stock market game that I bet some of you didn't know about. Don't just take my word for it, get in touch with your 401k advisor today and ask them what you are invested in.

# CHAPTER 7:

# FAQ
## *[STOCK TRADING]*

S o many people don't know where to begin or what questions to ask when it comes to stock trading. We have done the hard part by researching the top questions asked by individuals wanting to trade.

Here are the top 10 most frequently many questions for beginners looking to start investing in the stock market.

**Question 1:**
How can I make money in the stock market? There are plenty of ways to make money in the stock market. Most people think that buying stocks and waiting for it to appreciate or collecting dividends are the only ways to make money. You can also rent stocks, sell stocks you don't own, and even profit off fallen stocks.

**Question 2:**

How soon will I begin to make money? It's possible to make a lot of money immediately by following tight parameters for trading. You will need to set up a trading account and establish these parameters. Due to volatility, you will incur a loss from time to time but in the long run, you will make money.

**Question 3:**

What's the difference between trading stocks yourself and having a stock broker do it for you? While it may be easier to let someone do it for you, you're losing out on money. Allowing a third party, a broker, or a trader, to trade on your behalf subjects you to additional fees. Not to mention, many investors use side strategies that may not be in your best interest but will help ensure that they make a bigger profit from your dollar.

**Question 4:**

How much money do I need to start? I recommend $100 but you can start off with less. This will allow you to realize some actual gains while assessing your risk tolerance.

**Question 5:**

How do I decide which companies to invest in? Do your research. There are countless ways to do research. It is mostly a combination of personal preference and the amount of capital at your disposal. From a research standpoint, a good place to start will be a fundamental analysis and technical analysis strategies. These strategies are important and we will touch on them later.

## Question 6:

What's the benefit of trading, versus savings, versus 401k? When you trade you can generate an ample amount of income. A savings account does not yield any interest worth mentioning. A 401k is market-dependent so your success depends solely on market performance. Historically, the market experiences a crash every decade leaving investors in a tough spot. As a trader, however, you can make money even when the market is down.

## Question 7:

Will I make money buying penny stocks? It is possible though not likely, therefore, we at www.MB-University.com do not recommend it. You're better off playing the lottery.

## Question 8:

How can I protect my money? The best way to protect your money is to invest it yourself. Learn about bonds and ETFs which are more secure than general stocks.

## Question 9:

What is shorting a stock? Shorting is just the opposite of buying a stock. You are profiting from the loss of a particular stock. And the final but most frequently asked question,

## Question 10:

What exactly is the stock market? The stock market is a place where companies go to raise capital for their business and in return, they offer a small fraction of the company's worth. If you have additional questions, feel free to contact me at www.MB-University.com.

# CHAPTER 8:

# GETTING STARTED
## *[STOCK TRADING]*

T he first thing you will need to do is set up a trading account. I recommend you do some research on the different platforms available that suits your needs. Some platforms provide research tools and education but charge higher fees. Other platforms have cheaper fees but provide no education and little to no research tools.

There's an ample amount of free research tools online that you can find to help you on your journey. Search a list of brokerage platforms that's right for you. When starting out, I recommend going with a cheaper platform since there plenty of free online research tools.

When registering they will ask a ton of questions about your trading experience to make sure you can afford to invest. Don't be intimidated, answer the questions to the best of your ability. Remember, stocks are also known as equity trade.

If given an option, apply for stocks also known as equity trading along with tier 1 options trading. In later chapters, I will discuss how to secure your stock picks by purchasing options. Once you have set up your account transfer 10% of your 1 month's pay to the account. Select 5 stocks you have a good feeling about and buy 1 share of each.

Don't rush into buying a lot of shares. Give yourself 2 weeks to a month to get used to the market fluctuation. Now don't forget, do your research on these 5 stocks. You should be able to give me good 3 reasons you believe each stock is worth investing in.

Be sure to add diversity in your picks. When I say diversity, I mean choose stocks from different sectors. For example, you have a financial sector, a technology sector, a natural gas sector, a retail sector, and the list goes on and on. Diversity prevents an investor from losing all their money if a company or industry collapse. For example, the oil industry has been depreciating in value but the technology industry is booming.

The biggest part of your research will be looking at the fundamental and technical analysis of a company. We will explore that further in later chapters. Just know a financial analyst has already rated the fundamentals of these companies and made it available online. So, the hard part of looking at companies' financials is already done.

If they have a good rating from an analyst and you believe in the company's future growth or upcoming product, don't be afraid to invest. Remember, the hardest part of investing is getting started.

# CHAPTER 9:

# SELECTING THE RIGHT STOCKS

## *[STOCK TRADING]*

I n order to select the right stocks, you have to familiarize yourself with stock screeners. A stock screener is a straightforward way to filter through thousands of stocks listed on a stock exchange. When using a stock screener, it is best to consider your own financial situation.

**You can choose from a variety of criteria:**

- Find a stock below a certain price
- Find a stock above a certain price
- Find a stock that has made good money within the last year
- Find a stock that has been rated A1 by the different analysts

- Find stocks that pay dividends

Creating your own criteria and learning how to use various stocks screeners is a fundamental step in acquiring wealth in the stock market. Once you have narrowed the selection of stocks down by using a stock screener, make sure the stock you choose is one that you believe in.

You may like their current product, you may like what they are working on, maybe they have a product or a prototype that's coming out in the future. Whatever it maybe you must believe in the long-term future of the company. When selecting the right stocks do not shy away from the pricier stocks even though they may be more expensive and you may not be able to buy as many shares, they often exhibit bigger and faster growth than the cheaper stocks. Stay within your means. Don't get caught keep up with the Jones'!

Be open to stocks of different price ranges. They will also help to diversify your portfolio and secure your money in the long run.

# CHAPTER 10:

# INTRO TO FUNDAMENTAL ANALYSIS
## *[STOCK TRADING]*

Fundamentals comprise of many various aspects from earning reports, to Federal Interest Rate announcement, to television news reports. The most important aspect of fundamental analysis is a company's financials.

This comprises of the company's income statements, balance sheets, and cash flow analysis. You will find many different equations such as profitability formulas, debt to income ratios and even operational cycle formulas.

These financial formulas can tell you a lot about a company but who has the time to dig deep through these companies' financials? True, it is the foundation of a company's success but let the people who are paid to comb through these numbers do their jobs.

Financial analysts rate companies according to their financials and the companies with the best ratings are the companies you want to invest in for the long-term. It's a requirement that any company that's publicly traded make its financials available to the public. So, if you want, feel free to go to a company's website and look up how the company is investing their money.

You also have the ability to listen into conference calls if you wish. Strong financial fundamentals are the foundation of any stock. Other news and events can move the price value of a stock but in the long run stocks with good fundamentals will always bounce back from bad news and appreciate in price. Always remember, pick the stocks with good fundamentals.

# CHAPTER 11:

# INTRO TO TECHNICAL ANALYSIS
## [STOCK TRADING]

T echnical analysis is very important because it gives you an idea of a company's past performance. A key theory in technical analysis is that history has and tends to repeat itself.

Formations and patterns give insight on what buyers and seller's next move might be. The 3 key parameters are trend line, support line, and resistance lines. Trend lines show you if the stock is growing, standing still, or losing money. It also shows you in what timeframe it took the stock to make a profit or a loss. The support line is often known as the floor. It is a line that the stock falls to and bounce off of to move back up. This is a level that is retested more than once throughout a certain timeframe.

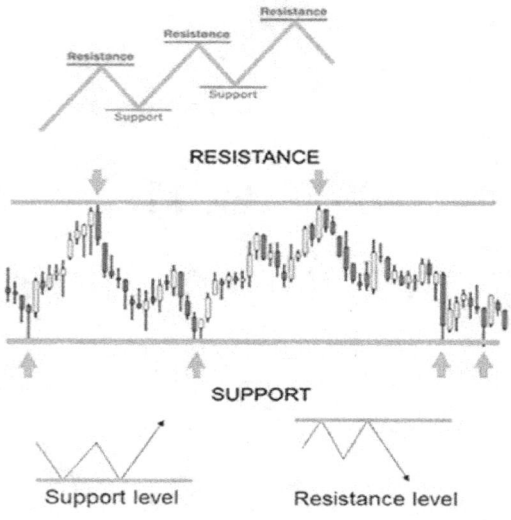

**RESISTANCE**

**SUPPORT**

Support level          Resistance level

The support line is the lower level line which is also known as the floor. The graph touches and retest this level and often bounces up from this line. There are some instances where the graph falls below this line. The resistance line is the upper level line also known as the ceiling. The graph touches and retest this level and often bounces down from this line. There are some instances where the graph soar above this line.

The resistance level or ceiling is a level that the stock price reaches but always seems to dip back down once it gets to that level. The resistance is often reached without breakthrough unless some good news like high earnings or big trade deal is secured.

You typically want to buy at the support and sell at the resistance. Keeping track of multiple stocks support and resistance levels can be difficult so my suggestion is to only familiarize yourself with 2 or 3 stocks.

Once you get the hang of identifying the trend line, the support line, and the resistance line MB-University will teach you to trade options effectively for income.

# CHAPTER 12:

# PLACING YOUR FIRST ORDERS
## [STOCK TRADING]

W hen places orders, you have a list of options that can be a benefit to your trading strategy. Here is a list of the most commonly used order types for beginners.

Market orders, limit orders, stop-loss orders, stop-limit orders, and trailing-stop orders.

**Market order**: the current price a particular stock is going for at this very point in time in the market. If you place this type of order it will be executed as soon as you press submit. The benefit is you will get in the market right away but the drawback is that you could have gotten it at a cheaper rate using a limit order.

**Limit order**: a price you can set so that your broker knows that this is the maximum amount of money that you're willing to pay for per share of a particular stock. The drawback to this is that you might miss the opportunity to buy the stock.

**Stop-loss order**: a protection order you can set to ensure that you won't lose more than you're willing to lose on a particular trade. The drawback to this is that if the stock has a huge drop, known as the gap down, your stock target can be missed and you can incur a bigger loss than anticipated.

**Stop-limit**: similar to a stop-loss, is a target profit order. You can set this order up when you have a good idea of how much money you want to make on a particular trade. The drawback to this is that you can potentially miss more profit if the stock continues to go up.

**Trailing stop**: is an order where your stop loss move upwards as the stock price move upwards. The stop loss will never move down in order to secure the profit you've incurred from the upward move. You can set your trailing stop at $1 below the stock price. If the stock moves up, let's say $52 to $53, your trailing stop will move up from $51 to $52 ensuring that don't lose more than $1 from the high point of the stock. The drawback is the same as the stop-loss, you can miss your trailing stop on a gap down of the stock price.

It's important to know how to use these market orders. Once you get more advanced you can use a combination of these orders to automate your trade without having to watch them. As a beginner, stick to placing market or limit orders.

When starting to invest it is important that you see a positive return on your money to ensure you stick with the process. Once you get more familiar with the market you can begin to take full advantage of the market swings.

# CHAPTER 13:

# WHEN TO BUY
## *[STOCK TRADING]*

People often ask me. "When should I buy a particular stock?" No one can time the market perfectly but experienced traders look for two things: an undervalued good company; or a dip in a good company's stock price.

A good undervalued company is one that is profitable and growing with a good product. Due to this company's good financials and product base, it will bounce back from dips in the market. So, with this being said, we look to buy on those dips. This ensures that you get the stock for a cheaper rate. As the stock keeps dipping you keep buying more as it reduces the overall cost you've paid for the stock. Once they recover you will see a nice profit and you can consider selling your shares if you wish.

There are many factors that can cause a company to dip. Make sure to do your research to see if it's a recoverable situation. When researching the dips, you will find people using technical and fundamental analysis. Some people even use indicators like RSI to see if the stock is overbought or oversold.

Don't get too deep in all of these different methods. It may confuse you and prevent you from making any kind of move. When you see a dip in the stock price ask yourself this question, is it a good company with good products and good financials? If so, don't be afraid to take the risk. Create yourself a simple strategy around this question.

## A Simple Strategy I use for long term investing:

- Is it between the range of $5 - $20?
- Is the stock Market Cap above 100 Million?
- Did it recently come out of penny stock range which is from $0 - $10?
- Has the stock grown 30% or better in the last quarter?
- Does the stock have an uptrend line for the past year or so?

Be sure to consider your budget along with personal goals. This will give you the confidence to place a winning trade.

There are many factors that can cause a company to dip. Make sure to do your research to see if it's a recoverable situation. When researching the dips, you will find people using technical and fundamental analysis. Some people even use indicators like RSI to see if the stock is overbought or oversold.

Don't get too deep in all of these different methods. It may confuse you and prevent you from making any kind of move. When you see a dip in the stock price ask yourself this question, is it a good company with good products and good financials? If so, don't be afraid to take the risk. Create yourself a simple strategy around this question. Be sure to consider your budget along with personal goals. This will give you the confidence to place a winning trade.

# CHAPTER 14:

# OPTIONS 101
## *[OPTION TRADING]*

Options trading officially began in 1973. So, in comparison to traditional stock trading, options are still fairly new. Option trading seems complicated to many investors, new and old, but it's actually quite simple.

## What are options?

Simply put, it's a contract to control 100 shares of a particular stock at a particular price for a particular amount of time.

## What are the benefit of options?

Options are extremely cheap in comparison to purchasing the stock outright. An option contract is less than 10% of the money required to purchase 100 shares of the same stock. It's roughly around 3-5% but can increase and decrease due to time, volatility and strike price. We'll touch on the specifics later but in general, it's cheaper.

## So, what does all this mean?

It means if you like a stock and you think it will be profitable within a certain timeframe, you can buy an option contract to control 100 shares for a small amount of money.

Here is an example. Let's say Nike is trading at $50 per share. You feel like Nike is doing something innovative with their shoes so you decide to purchase a call option contract at a strike price of $50. We will get to terminologies soon but for clarity, buy a call means you're bullish, a strike call means the reference or the base price of the stock.

Let's assume this option cost $300 and it is good for 3 months. If the buyer's assumption is correct and Nike's stock goes to let's say $60 per share the buyer has just made $10 per share. Remembering that each contract is worth 100 shares, 100 x 10 = $1,000.

The cost of the contract is $300 so the overall profit will be $700. This does not take into account the cost of the trading fees your broker, like E trade or Capital One, may charge you.

What if the buyer's assumption is incorrect and the stock goes in the opposite direction within the 3 months' timeframe?

The buyer just lost the entire $300. Because of this, although cheaper than buying outright, many say options are riskier. You have the ability to lose the entire amount of your investment if you guess incorrectly.

Options consist of two main components, calls and puts. Buying a call option means you have the reason to believe the stock value of a particular stock is going up. On the other hand, buying a put means you have reason to believe the stock value of a particular stock is going down.

I've given you an example of a call purchase. Here's an example of a put purchase. Let's say I own Nike and it's still trading at $50 per share. I own 100 shares but due to the bad company news I predict the value will decrease soon. I buy 1 put contract for $200. This contract ensures that if the stock price falls below $50 I will still be able to sell it at $50 per share. This contract acts as insurance if I own the stock.

Let's say Nike falls to $40 per share. This contract ensures that the seller of the contract must pay me $50 per share for my stock. I only lose what I paid for the contract which is $200. But what if I don't own the stock but I brought this put contract anyway because I predicted the stock price was going to fall? What your broker would do on your behalf is purchase the stock in the market at $40 per share and then sell it to whoever you have the contract agreement with at $50 per share, giving you a $1,000 gain.

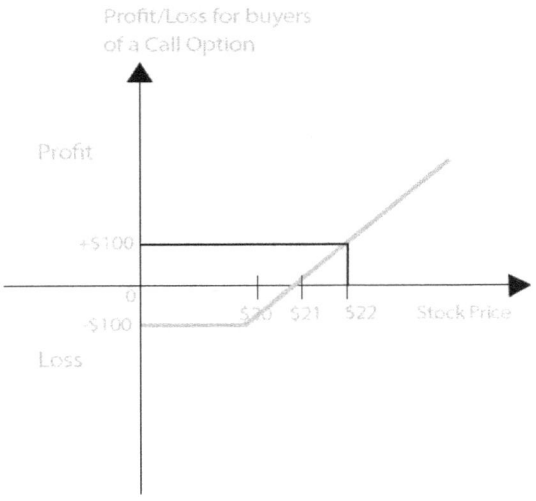

This call option shows a buyer paying $100 as a premium for 1 call option of a particular stock that's currently trading at $20. Remember 1 call option is worth 100 shares. Once the stock moves up 1 point, to $21 dollars, the graph shows you breaking even. You paid $100 and you made $100 so your profit is at $0. It's not until you get above $21 when you start to see a profit. If the stock is trading at $22, you made $100 in profit minus fees and etc.

When you take into consideration that this contract is worth $1,000 that $1,000 gain minus the $200 you paid for the contract, $800 is the profit on this contract minus the broker fees for the trade. Similar to the previous example, if the put goes in the opposite direction, as in upwards, you lose the entire premium of $200.

# CHAPTER 15:

# TERMINOLOGY
## *[OPTION TRADING]*

Now, let us get familiar with some terms. Options, by definition, is the right but not the obligation to buy a particular stock or security for a set price also known as the strike before or at the time of expiration. The buyer of the option contract pays a premium. The seller receives the premium.

When trading options you can choose to be a buyer or a seller. What does all this mean? Its means, is that if you're a buyer, the person that pays the premium, you have the right to execute the terms of the contract if it's to your benefit, of course.

If you are the seller, the person receiving the premium, you do not have a choice but to honor a contract, whether it's for your benefit or not because you're paid a premium to do so. Your contract could be to buy or sell a security at a certain price known as the strike.

Let's get some clarification. Here's a rundown of important terminology now that we know what options are.

**Strike price:**
The agreed upon price at which the stock will be bought or sold.

**The Premium:**
The price the buyer of the contract pays to the seller of the contract.

**The expiration:**
The date the option agreement expires.

These are key elements of option contracts but before you can make a decision on these elements you have to choose a position. You do this by using either a call or a put or a combination of the two.

As previously mentioned, a Call means to go up. Put means to go down. So, if I buy a call, I think the stock is going up on bullish. If I buy a put, I think the stock is going down on bearish. Notice I use the word buy in both of these scenarios. I am the buyer, the one that pays the premium. What if I'm the seller? It's the exact opposite. If I sell a call I think the stock is going down I'm bearish. If I sell a put I think the stock is going up I'm bullish. Picking one of these positions will help you determine if you're in the money, at the money, or out the money.

**In the money:**
When a strike is below the current trading price of a call or when the price is above the current trading price of a put.

**Out the money:**
When a strike is above the current trading price of a call or when the price is below the current trading price of a put.

**At the money:**
The closest to strike prices which the stock is trading between.

Remember, in the money, out the money, and out the money changes depending on what position you are taking.

The term execute means to take possession of the stock for the agreed upon strike price.

Selling the Contract. You can sell the contract instead of executing it. If there's no real interest in owning it, just sell it for the profit.

**Intrinsic value:**
In the money only which has the difference of the strike price and the current trading price value factored in a premium.

**Extrinsic value:**
The value of time and volatility factored into the premium.

**Delta:**
The profit made per dollar or point movement.

**Theta:**
Time decay. If you're buying, time works against you, and if you're selling, time works in your favor.

**Gamma:**
Measures the rate of change in delta for each point movement in an underlying security.

**Volatility:**
Measures the fluctuation in an underlying asset.

**Vega:**
Measures the sensitivity of the price of an option to changes and volatility.

The term covered means, you own the stock.

Naked means, you don't own the stock.

Leverage means you control more with a little.

Margin means, the money used to cover a loss of a position.

Terms can vary by brokers so be sure to familiarize yourself with these terms and other terms used in trading. The Greek terminology is often used in more advance applications of option trading. Further your education in options before you begin to trade it for income.

# CHAPTER 16:

# INTRO TO OPTIONS
## *[OPTION TRADING]*

Options are contracts that give you leverage. Remember leverage is the ability to control a lot with a little. One contract is worth 100 shares and that contract cost is less than 10% of the cost required to buy the stock.

Option contracts are similar to renting stock. You can take control of the stock of your choice at a certain price. Let me give you an example. Let's say you want to buy an Apple option contract because you feel the latest iPhone is going to do well. Apple is trading at $90 per share so you buy the option at a strike price of $90.

The strike price is the price which will take control of the stock. The contract cost you $100 which is also known as the premium. There is a one-month expiration on this contract which means you will own this contract for only one month.

If the stock does well and moves to $100 per share, you just made $10 per share because you took control of it at $90 per share. $10 x the 100 shares you own = $1,000. You must subtract the $100 that you paid, so you made $900 in profit.

If the stock goes down due to poor sales you lose the $100 premium that you paid. Options are considered to be riskier because you can lose 100% of the $100 you invested but with a proper education you can utilize this leverage tool to get rich.

What you need to understand is that investing in options is not for everyone. Know the risks before you trade. Investing are for those with disposable income and that are willing to take a bigger risk for a bigger reward.

# CHAPTER 17:

# GETTING STARTED IN OPTIONS TRADING
## *[OPTION TRADING]*

The first step in trading options is to pick 3 volatile stock. I recommend choosing from the S&P 500. The S&P 500 is the top 500 American companies and their daily overall cumulative profitability index. The reasons I say to choose from these stocks are because they're heavily traded and more stable than smaller companies. So, choose your 3 favorites that have pretty good price movement.

Once you figure out the 3 you like, sit back and watch it for a month or two. As previously mentioned, you want to use technical analysis to determine the support and resistance. Once that is determined, you can begin to start placing trades.

At the determined support, buy one call option for an expiration of six6 to eight8 weeks. At the determined resistance, buy one put option for an expiration of six (6) to eight (8) weeks. Do not shoot for full profit because the profit can be endless but the losses can be as well.

Shoot for a 50% profit until you get the hang of trading options then you can adjust your profit margins according to your goals. If a call option costs $100, your profit taking should be at $150 with $50 being your profit. This is a good starting point for trading options.

The hardest part of trading options is one, waiting for the perfect opportunity to place your trade and two, not becoming too greedy. Options trading really depends on the control of emotions. If you are an emotional person stick with the buy and hold philosophy of trading. If you aren't an emotional person, make sure you create a strategy to stay on track.

# CHAPTER 18:

# CREATING A STRATEGY
## [OPTION TRADING]

Your strategy will depend on personal factors such as how much money can you invest, how much of this investment are you willing to lose, how much time do you want to spend in a trade, how much growth are you looking for, how much time do you have to put towards trading? These are all important questions to help you select the appropriate stocks and timeframe for holding a particular position.

Here is an example. Let's say you only have $100 and you're looking to make some good growth, you can pick a cheap call option like GoPro which may cost you $60. If GoPro has a good earnings announcement, this can double the $60 to $120 but if GoPro has a bad announcement, it can turn that $60 into $5. These are investments that carry high risks, especially when you choose a time frame of one month or less.

For the trader that wants less risk, he or she can sell out the money contracts for income. You make around 4-10% of your investments but it carries less risk if done properly. Earnings or news events will be something to watch out for because it can really affect the price movement.

Choosing fewer volatile stocks also help to keep you protected from risk. Remember, choosing small timeframes is to your benefits when selling. These are all strategies.

Other popular strategies are trading on earning, trading on indicators, trading on fundamentals. Whatever you choose to trade by, just make sure it fits your budget and that you stick to your methods. As time progresses, you will have to tweak these strategies to make sure it's perfect for your lifestyle.

# CHAPTER 19:

# INSURING YOUR STOCK WITH OPTIONS
## [OPTION TRADING]

Options can benefit every type of trader. Maybe trading options isn't for you. You may not want to make speculative decisions on whether a stock is going up or down, maybe you like a specific company and want to invest in it. You can buy shares of stock and purchase a put option for a premium to secure a price you will be able to cash stock out for, but it must be in multiples of 100 because one1 option contract represents 100 shares.

For example, you own a stock that' is $30 per share, you have 100 shares valued at which equate to $3,000. You believe the stock is going to go up but you're not sure. what's going to happen with new laws that might limit the company's ability to sell its product. You can buy a put contract at a strike price of $30 per share for a specific period of time that guarantees if the stock drops below $30 per share, maybe to $24 per share, the contract guarantees that you will still be paid $30 per share during the period of the contract. You can then sell your shares at $30 per share to the contract owner and go rebuy the same shares at the market for $24 per share, giving you $600 profit minus the premium and any other trading fees.

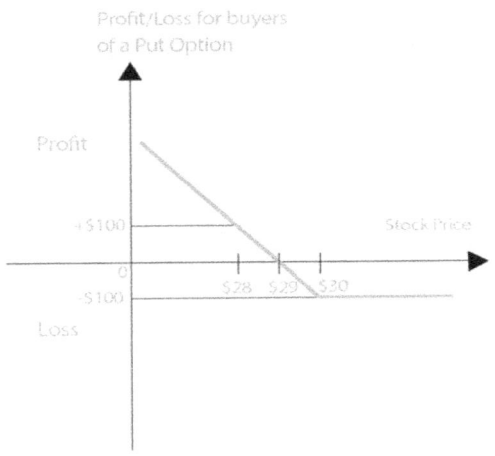

This put option shows a buyer paying $100 as a premium for 1 put option of a particular stock that's currently trading at $30. Remember 1 call option is worth 100 shares. Once the stock moves down 1 point, to $29 dollars, the graph shows you breaking even. You paid $100 and you made $100 so your profit is at $0. It's not until you get below $29 when you start to see a profit. If the stock is trading at $28, you made $100 in profit minus fees and etc.

The point is, options can be a benefit to all types of traders. Invest in your education today with www.MB-University.com and learn which strategies are best for you.

# CONCLUSION

T hank you for reading this book. It shows you are ready to make the best investment is investing in yourself and learning secrets to making your money grow. All too often, we take the easy and passive approach because life seems too busy to learn something new. This book has made it easy for you.

It's time to stop working so hard and start working smarter. The more you allow your money to work for you the more you can make time to do what you enjoy doing most. Whether it's golfing with friends, travelling, or spending time with family. Take control of your life by investing in you.

After reading this book, I am certain you are more aware of your financial situation and financial capabilities. Now it is up to you to consider your future goals and decide that you will be committed to reaching them. Work on being more disciplined with your spending and more productive in your investing.

I hope this book has given you a good foundation of knowing what to look for when selecting the right stock for your portfolio. Don't be afraid to pull the trigger on buying. If you have doubts, remember you can use Options as insurance. When trading stocks the best teacher is experience but while you're learning be sure to limit your risk by only investing a small amount of money until you feel you're ready to invest more. We encourage you to continue your education and take time to research your potential investments. Know all the risks before you trade. For additional information and education contact a professional today!

# GLOSSARY

**Assets:**
Anything tangible or intangible that can be owned or controlled to produce value and that is held by a company to produce positive economic value is an asset.

**At the money:**
If the current price and strike price are equal at expiration. Balance sheet also known as statement of financial position is a summary of the financial balances of an individual or organization Assets and liabilities.

**Bearish:**
If investors expect downward price movement in the stock market. Bonds-a debt security, under which the issuer owes the holders a debt and (depending on the terms of the bond) is obliged to pay them interest (the coupon) and/or to repay the principal at a later date.

**Bullish**: If investors expect upward price movement in the stock market. Broker -is an individual or company who arranges transactions between a buyer and a seller for a commission when the deal is executed.

**Buyer:** is any person who contracts to acquire an asset with some form of payment.

**Call Option**: Often simply labelled a "call", is a financial contract between two parties, the buyer and the seller of this type of option. [1] The buyer of the call option has the right, but not the obligation, to buy an agreed quantity of a particular commodity or financial instrument (the underlying) from the seller of the option at a certain time (the expiration date) for a certain price (the strike price). The seller (or "writer") is obligated to sell the commodity or financial instrument to the buyer if the buyer so decides. The buyer pays a fee (called a premium) for this right. The term "call" comes from the fact that the owner has the right to "call the stock away" from the seller.

**Cash flow**: Is mostly used to describe payments that are expected to happen in the future, are thus uncertain and therefore need to be forecasted with cash flows;

**Certificate of Deposit (CD's)**: Are similar to savings accounts in that they are insured "money in the bank" and thus virtually risk free. In the USA, summary of the financial balances of an individual or organization Assets and liabilities. CDs are insured by the Federal Deposit Insurance Corporation (FDIC) for banks and by the National Credit Union Administration (NCUA) for credit unions. They differ from savings accounts in that the CD has a specific, fixed term (often one, three, or six months, or one to five years and, usually, a fixed interest rate. The bank intends that the customer hold the CD until maturity, at which time they can withdraw the money and accrued interest.

**Credit**: Is the trust which allows one party to provide money or resources to another party where that second party does not reimburse the first party immediately (thereby generating a debt, but instead promises either to repay or return those resources (or other materials of equal value at a later date.

**Covered** - Is a financial market transaction in which the seller owns the corresponding amount of the underlying instrument, such as shares of a stock.

**Delta**: Measures the rate of change of the theoretical option value with respect to changes in the underlying asset's price.

Dividends -a payment made by a corporation to its shareholders, usually as a distribution of profits.

**Equity**: The difference between the value of the assets and the value of the liabilities of something owed. This term is often used to refer to stocks.

**ETF**: An exchange traded fund which operates on the stock market an represent a group of stock and/or a particular sector.

**Execute or Exercise**: The financial transaction specified by the contract is to be carried out immediately between the two parties, whereupon the option contract is terminated.

**Expiration**: This is the date on which the option expires, or becomes worthless, if the buyer doesn't exercise it.

**Extrinsic value**: The value of time and volatility factored into the premium.

**Federal Reserve**: Often known as the Feds is the central banking system of the United States created in 1913 to help regulate the economy through monetary policy. The term monetary policy refers to the actions undertaken by a central bank, such as the Federal Reserve, to influence the availability and cost of money and credit to help promote national economic goals usually by way of interest rates.

**Forex**: The foreign exchange market (Forex, FX, or currency market is a global decentralized or over-the-counter (OTC market for the trading of currencies.

**Futures**: A standardized forward contract, a legal agreement to buy or sell something at a predetermined price at a specified time in the future. Fundamental analysis - the analysis of a business's financial statements to determine its financial health.

**Gamma**: Measures the rate of change in the delta with respect to changes in the underlying price.

**Income statement**: The purpose of the income statement is to show managers and investors whether the company made or lost money (revenues - expenses during the period being reported).

**In the money**: If the derivative would make money if it were to expire today.

**Intrinsic value**: In the money only, which has the difference of the strike price and the current trading price value factored in a premium.

**Leverage:** Any technique involving the use of borrowed funds in the purchase of an asset, with the expectation that the after-tax income from the asset and asset price appreciation will exceed the borrowing cost.

**Limit Order**: an order to buy a security at no more than a specific price, or to sell a security at no less than a specific price.

**Margin**: Collateral that the holder of a financial instrument has to deposit with a counterparty (most often their broker or an exchange to cover some or all of the credit risk the holder poses for the counterparty.

**Market Order:** A buy or sell order to be executed immediately at current market prices.

**Mutual Fund**: A professionally managed investment fund that pools money from many investors to purchase securities. Mutual funds have advantages and disadvantages compared to direct investing in individual securities. The primary advantages of mutual funds are that they provide a higher level of diversification, they provide liquidity, and they are managed by professional investors. On the negative side, investors in a mutual fund must pay various fees and expenses.

**Naked**: Is where the seller does not hold the underlying position to cover the contract in case of assignment.

**Out the money** - if the derivative would not make money if it were to expire today.

**Premium**: This is the price you pay when you buy an option and the price you receive when you sell an option.

**Position**: To be bullish or bearish or a buyer or a seller.

**Put Option**: A stock market device which gives the owner of a put the right, but not the obligation, to sell an asset (the underlying, at a specified price (the strike, by a predetermined date (the expiry or maturity to a given party (the seller of the put. The purchase of a put option is interpreted as a negative sentiment about the future value of the underlying. [1] The term "put" comes from the fact that the owner has the right to "put up for sale" the stock or index.

**Stock screener**: Systematic stock picking methods that utilize computer software and/or data.

**Sector:** Based on similar production processes, similar products, or similar behavior in financial mark.

**Seller**: The provider of the goods or services for compensation. Shorting - the practice of selling securities or other financial instruments that are not currently owned (usually borrowed, and subsequently repurchasing them ("covering". In the event of an interim price decline, the short seller profits, since the cost of (repurchase is less than the proceeds received upon the initial (short sale. Conversely, the short position closes out at a loss if the price of a shorted instrument rises prior to repurchase.

**Stock**: Also known as security or equity stock of its owners. A single share of the stock represents fractional ownership of the corporation in proportion to the total number of shares.

**Stop limit order**: Combines the features of a stop order and a limit order. Once the stop price is reached, the stop–limit order becomes a limit order to buy (or to sell at no more (or less than another, per-specified limit price. [13] As with all limit orders, a stop-limit order doesn't get filled if the security's price never reaches the specified limit price.

**Stop loss order**: A protection order you can set to ensure that you won't lose more than you're willing to lose on a particular trade. Strike price – this is the price at which you can buy the stock (if you have bought a call option) or the price at which you must sell your stock (if you have sold a call option).

**Technical analysis**: An analysis methodology for forecasting the direction of prices through the study of past market data, primarily price and volume.

**Theta** - Measures the sensitivity of the value of the derivative to the passage of time.

**Trailing stop order**: Is entered with a stop parameter that creates a moving or trailing activation price, hence the name. This parameter is entered as a percentage change or actual specific amount of rise (or fall in the security price. Trailing stop sell orders are used to maximize and protect profit as a stock's price rises and limit losses when its price falls.

**Trend line:** Is a bounding line for the price movement of a security.

**Vega**: Measures sensitivity to volatility.

**Volatility**: The degree of variation of a trading price series over time. 401k - defined-contribution pension account defined in subsection 401k of the Internal Revenue Code. [1] Under the plan, retirement savings contributions are provided (and sometimes proportionately matched by an employer, deducted from the employee's paycheck before taxation) (therefore tax-deferred until withdrawn after retirement or as otherwise permitted by applicable law, and limited to a maximum pre-tax annual contribution of $18,000 as of 2017.)

# ABOUT THE AUTHOR

My name is Michael A. Bempah. I was born and raised on the Southside of Chicago, in the Englewood community. As a child, I saw how hard my parents worked to provide for our family. I knew, from a very young age, I wanted to do more than just "provide". Failure wasn't an option. Like a lot of young black men, I grew up with others telling me I wouldn't be able to accomplish the level of success I desired. Fortunately, my determination and resilience led to many accomplishments.

I graduated from Southern Illinois University-Carbondale with a B.S. in Civil Engineering and minor in Mathematics. After college, I worked for

The Illinois Department of Transportation (IDOT). At IDOT, I managed various projects in the field. After acquiring the necessary experience and passing all the required examinations, I became an Illinois licensed Professional Engineer.

Every day, I worked endlessly doing exactly what I swore I would never do. I was working day in and day out to simply "provide".

This wasn't the life I wanted for myself. True, I was making decent money but the old saying still holds true, "the more money you make, the more problems you will have". I had to change the way I was programmed to think about money. Once I changed my mindset, I realized, I could make a substantial amount of money with any income. I enrolled in a professional stock trading course and began applying what I learned. I was able to earn enough money from my moves in the stock market to leave IDOT and start my own engineering firm. I am committed to teaching my community the fundamentals of stock trading. I want you to learn everything you can from this easy to read guide in creating generational wealth for you and your family.

Learn More at www.MB-University.com